A souvenir guide

Tudor Merchant's House

Pembrokeshire

Amy Feldman

🍂 **National Trust**

A Town Built on the Sea

Tucked down a narrow Norman alley within Tenby's walls lies the Tudor Merchant's House – the town's oldest unaltered building – and a place that transports you to 1500.

Tenby is a small town, yet somehow it's still easy to lose yourself here down curving, Norman streets; along walkways clutching the edge of Castle Hill; on the sweeping stretch of sand below South Beach's ice-cream coloured Victorian hotel buildings.

Wherever you find yourself, it is never far from the sea: a deep turquoise reminiscent of the Mediterranean in summer, in winter it provides a dramatic spectacle as clouds tumble over headland and turn the water silver-blue.

It is the sea, and Tenby's proximity to it, that made the town its fortune twice over. Most recently this was as a fashionable Victorian beach resort, which remains popular with holidaymakers today (so much so that the area inside the town walls is closed to vehicles without a valid permit). Five hundred years earlier, Tenby was a busy, commercial Tudor trading port that made successful merchants of many – including the resident of Tudor Merchant's House.

Experiencing Tudor Merchant's House today

Today, Tudor Merchant's House replicates – as much as possible – the home of one such middle-class, wealthy Merchant. It is not exactly the same building that he would have lived in; the stairs have moved indoors, room boundaries have changed and windows have been replaced. Much of the furniture and objects are authentic replicas, rather than original Tudor pieces. Despite this, as soon as you step through the oak front door into the former trading area, you are transported back 500 years: to a time when servants prepared meals around a constantly-crackling fireplace; when the main meal of the day was the perfect opportunity to show off your status; when one family shared just a single bedchamber.

Uncovering the former residents

Many details of the Merchant's family remain a mystery – the only record of an inhabitant from this time is Thomas Jurdan, who rented the house in the 1580s for two shillings and sixpence a year. Yet Thomas also owned 17 other properties in the medieval town and just outside, so it's unlikely he actually ever lived here.

But based on what we know about life in Tudor Tenby, and clues discovered around the house, we can piece together a picture of the earlier Merchant and his wife: the goods they traded and the food they ate; how they entertained guests and raised their children, as well as their everyday activities. Objects placed around the house help bring these stories to life today.

Opposite Early morning at Tenby harbour. Tudor Merchant's House lies straight ahead, up the path between the yellow and pink houses. Before the development of the surrounding houses, it would have afforded views out to sea

Below A cutaway illustration of Tudor Merchant's House as it may have looked in the 15th century

Tenby Through Time

875   'In Praise of Tenby' poem written, the earliest known record of Tenby

1093   Normans arrive in Tenby

1100s   Normans build a castle to defend against attacks by the native Welsh

1153   Attack on Tenby Castle by Welsh forces. Most of the garrison is slaughtered

1200+   Tenby's walls first built

1220-34   St Mary's Church built by the Earl of Pembroke

1260   Llewelyn ap Gruffydd slaughters many residents and destroys the castle

1264   Castle rebuilt by the Earls of Pembrokeshire

1328   Tenby's first quay built

1329   Population of Tenby reaches approximately 1,500

1457   Jasper Tudor carries out extensive refortification of the Town

1471   The future King Henry VII escapes to France through Tenby with Jasper Tudor

1485   Henry VII ascends to the throne. The Tudor period begins

1490   Tudor Merchant's House built

1512   Mathematican Robert Recorde is born in Tenby

1581   A charter granted by Queen Elizabeth I incorporates the town under a 'mayor, bailiffs and burgesses of the borough of Tenby'

1585   Occupier of Tudor Merchant's House is known to be Thomas Jurdan, who owns 17 other properties in and around the town

1642   The English Civil War begins

1643   Tenby and its Castle garrisoned for Charles I

1644   Parliamentary forces take Tenby Castle following a three-day siege. Around three hundred prisoners are taken

Above The Tenby Coat of Arms as featured on the 'Ja-Ja' heraldic series of postcards by Stoddart & Co Ltd

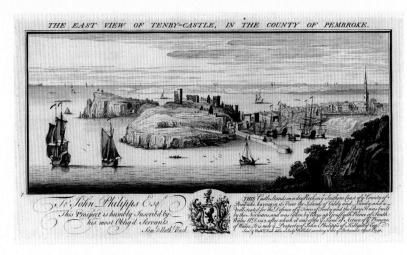

THE EAST VIEW OF TENBY-CASTLE, IN THE COUNTY OF PEMBROKE.

1647	Tenby Castle and the town seized for Charles I
1648	The Castle garrison revolts against Parliament, but surrender after three weeks' siege
1650–51	A devastating plague wipes out much of Tenby's population
1670	Population of Tenby is just 850
1800	Tudor Merchant's House wall paintings probably installed
1805	Sir William Paxton moves to Tenby and begins its regeneration
1810	Population of Tenby is around 800
1829	New market place built in the High Street
1830s	Population of Tenby is around 2,100
1852	The first lifeboat station is established (the first RNLI boathouse is established later, in 1862)
1869	The fort on top of St Catherine's Rock is built
1878	Tenby Museum & Art Gallery is established
1911	Population of Tenby reaches 4,368
1930	Council suggests funds raised to save Tudor Merchant's House
1938	Tudor Merchant's House is vested in the National Trust. Restoration work begins
1951	Tudor Merchant's House achieves Grade I listed status
1984	Additional restoration work takes place on Tudor Merchant's House

Above *The East View of Tenby Castle* by Samuel and Nathaniel Buck, 1740. Two of the most influential topographical artists of the 18th century, the Buck brothers created a record of over 500 ancient monuments and towns in England and Wales

Below left An engraving of Tenby lifeboat out in a storm, 1859

Below right *Caldey Island from Tenby Castle* by Henry Gastineau, 1835

The earliest days

Tenby's origins can be dated back almost 2,000 years, to a wooden hill fort atop Castle Hill.

In 410AD, the Romans abandoned Britain. What followed was a tumultuous period in the country's history. The English were at war with the Scots, attacked by the Saxons, and then devastated by Vikings. Wales, meanwhile, was fighting its own battles. The area was divided into 'petty kingdoms', each with their own 'kings' or 'princes'. Constantly at war with one another, these rulers squabbled over land and money.

The mysterious settlement

With all this fighting, protective hill forts were in order. It's believed there was one in Tenby and it is from this that the town's name originates – 'Tenby' derives from 'Dynbych', which means 'little fort'. The poem 'Edmyg Dinbych' ('The Praise of Tenby'), dating to around 875AD, is the first known mention of Tenby as a place. The anonymous author talks of a hill fortress 'safe above the sea', an 'unyielding stronghold' belonging to 'the head of Erbin's line'. The poet writes of bloody battles against enemies from the northern kingdom of Gwynedd, of men falling for their noble chief. But they also describe a place of comradery and soaring seabirds, merry men and festivals. Although no evidence of this fort remains, we think it could have been located on Castle Hill and made up of a series of wooden palisades, ditches and ramparts.

Around the same time, the Norse raided the Kingdom of Deheubarth (roughly south Wales, including Pembrokeshire) and it's thought some settled there. Their legacy can be seen in Scandinavian place names scattered around the region, from Caldey Island ('Cold Island') to Skomer (originally 'Skalmey' or 'Cleft Island'). It's probable that Tenby remained a mercantile settlement or hill fort until the late 11th century.

Norman Tenby

In 1093, Arnulf de Montgomery and his Norman army marched into South Pembrokeshire. With its fertile land and a powerful defensive position on the sea, the area's strategic importance was clear. Soon after, Tenby was captured. From the 12th to 15th centuries, the Normans crafted the rocky promontory into a town and replaced the fort with a castle, intended to protect the town from invasions by the native Welsh.

The town's early years were tumultuous. It was attacked in 1153 and again in 1187. The most devastating attack came in 1260: the castle was destroyed and many residents slaughtered in Llewelyn ap Gruffydd's sack of Tenby, part of his campaign to retake south Wales from the English for Gwynedd.

The Walls and Five Arches Gate

At this time, the town was under the control of the Earls of Pembroke, William and Joan de Valence. Realising Tenby needed better protection following an attack in 1260, they commissioned its fortification: thick, stone walls surrounding the town.

Although begun by the de Valences, the walls appear to have undergone five periods of construction, with later additions commissioned by Jasper Tudor (1457) and Queen Elizabeth I (1543–8). Five Arches is the medieval walls' only surviving gate today, but most Normans and Tudors would have entered Tenby through the 'Great Gate' or 'Carmarthen Gate' to the north, which was demolished in 1782.

Opposite The remains of Tenby castle, perched atop the highest point on Castle Hill. Almost surrounded by sea, it affords views of both North and South beach and, on a clear day, as far as Carmarthen Bay

Other Norman developments

It wasn't just the walls that were constructed during this period. St Mary's Church was begun sometime between 1220–34, probably built on the site of an earlier, 12th-century church. The castle was rebuilt in 1264, and it's the disconnected remains of this that can still be seen scattered around the town. On the former site of the castle itself now stands Tenby Museum & Art Gallery. It's thought the cobbled, winding lanes between the church and castle were also built around this time, and the triangular area outside Tudor Merchant's House may have been a small marketplace.

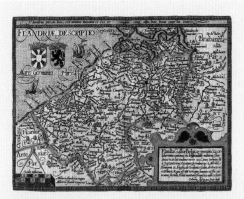

The Flemings

Following their conquest, the Normans wanted to squash the rebellious Welsh and consolidate their power. Allegedly they did so by introducing Flemings to the area, as well as Englishmen from the south-west.

Tudor Tenby

The Tudor period (1485–1603) was a prosperous one for England and Wales. Businesses boomed, levels of education and literacy soared and the country commanded global power. Mostly thanks to its trading links, Tenby became an important port.

The Tenby sailors

Dating from 1328, Tenby's quay was one of the earliest in Wales. But it was in the 15th and 16th centuries that Tenby became a truly busy port, its sailors travelling to Ireland, France, Portugal and Spain. They exported local coal and woollen cloth and returned home from Ireland with horses for ploughing, cattle, fish and iron, or laden with continental salt, wine, oil and dried fruit.

Others stayed closer to home; Tenby sailors were exempt from duties in Bristol's port. Barnstaple was another important route; they delivered wool and woollen cloth, hides, lambskins and tanned leather and brought back – amongst other items – groceries, soap, brass and pewter, and haberdashery. A case of Barnstaple ware pottery dating from the period, seemingly dumped outside the town walls and North Gate, now belongs to the Tenby Museum & Art Gallery collections.

Yet trading by sea could be a hazardous profession. Sailors fell foul of vicious storms, preying pirates and – should their ships come aground – pillaging.

Robert Recorde (1512–1558)

Renowned for inventing the 'equals' sign, mathematician Robert Recorde was born in Tenby in the early Tudor period. He was educated in a small school based in the town church and, aged 15, went on to study mathematics at the University of Oxford. About 20 years later he gained a second degree, in medicine, at Cambridge and went on to be physician to King Edward VI and Queen Mary.

Recorde published a number of works on maths but his most influential was *The Whetstone of Whitte*. Dating from 1557, this introduced algebra into Britain and contains the first use of the equals sign.

However, he picked his enemies unwisely, attempting to sue Sir William Herbert – later the Earl of Pembroke – for defamation of character. Herbert counter-sued and Recorde lost. When he didn't pay the subsequent and (substantial) fine, Recorde was arrested for debt and died in prison. A memorial to him can be seen in St Mary's Church.

Left A memorial to mathematician Robert Recorde, one of Tenby's most famous residents, inside St Mary's Church

Opposite The wall hanging of Jasper Tudor, depicting Tenby in the background, covers the back wall of the Hall Chamber inside Tudor Merchant's House

The escape of Henry VII

Henry VII (1457–1509) would become the first Tudor monarch, but his accession to the throne was not a simple one.

Born in Pembroke Castle, Henry was the only child of Edmund Tudor and a member of the Plantagenet Royal Family. His father died three months before Henry's birth, and as his mother was only 13, Henry VII was raised by his uncle, Jasper Tudor.

Henry was born two years after the start of the War of the Roses, a 32-year battle for the throne between the Plantagenets – the House of Lancaster – and the House of York. Although the House of Lancaster eventually won, they lost many earlier battles. In 1471 at the Battle of Tewkesbury, Edward IV won power for the House of York and many Lancastrians died or were executed as a result. Jasper and Henry escaped to safety in France, departing from Tenby harbour.

It's thought the pair hid in the cellars of the White family, good friends of Jasper Tudor who lived on the High Street where Boots the chemist now sits. They escaped through underground tunnels leading down to the sea and made it to France by boat, living in safety until Edward IV's death in 1483. Their escape is depicted on a colourfully painted cloth in the Hall Chamber.

 The superstitious Tudors
Seafaring

- As salt was thought to be lucky, it was said never to part with it at sea
- Cats were a sign of bad luck. If a sailor saw a cat on the way to the dock, they shouldn't sail
- It was best not to whistle on board a ship as you might cause a storm: to whistle was to try and rival the wind itself.
- Egg shells were broken into tiny pieces to stop witches sailing in them

Exploring Tudor Merchant's House

Dating from 1490, Tudor Merchant's House is the oldest – and only – complete surviving building of its type in Tenby. It transports visitors back to an earlier time, when it was the home of a wealthy Merchant and his family.

The exterior

When asked to describe a typically Tudor house, many might think of picturesque black-and-white wooden structures. However, in Tenby most of the buildings were made of stone, as it was quarried from nearby cliffs and transported to the town by sea. The exterior of the house also features an unusual round chimneystack; such designs seem to appear on a small number of medieval Pembrokeshire houses.

The Trading Area

You would have smelled this room before you saw it: sweet cinnamon and the earthy tang of cloves; spicy ginger and rich, fine wines – all ready to be traded with those who stepped into this crowded front room.

Like today, the Merchant would have greeted visitors from behind a large, colourful desk scattered with bills, payment records and notes of items brought in and out. Goods were proudly displayed, to tempt visitors to go on to the harbour where they could purchase them from little huts. Each product was labelled with a unique measurement: fardels of cloth sat alongside kilterkins of butter, stones of cheese next to hogsheads of imported wines. There may also have been fruit alongside hides and skins.

But there were three items in particular that would have made the Merchant rich: wool, salt and spices. Wool was a popular British export, salt was used as a food preservative, and spices covered the taste of the salt or food that perhaps was not as fresh as hoped for. The most valuable was nutmeg – a 14th-century German price tag revealed that one pound of the spice cost the same as 'seven fat oxen'. At the time, it was the Portuguese who held a monopoly over a small group of Indonesian islands from which nutmeg came, making it a rare, and therefore a highly expensive commodity.

Left The exterior of Tudor Merchant's House, tucked down a cobbled alley in the centre of Tenby. The harbour lies just to the west

What would the room have looked like?

The Tudors loved colour, and the room would have burst with yellows, greens and golds, as it does today. It would have been a similar size too, but the back wall wouldn't have been the same one; this was installed in the late 18th or early 19th century. It's possible this room and the kitchen beyond (see page 12) were divided, but by a wooden compartment.

The floor – which was probably made of bedrock filled with crushed shale and mortar – was lined with a woven rush mat, an upgrade to the straw and sweet herbs strewn here in previous years. It would also have been about fifty centimetres lower than it is today; it was raised in the 19th century, which is why rocks can be seen at the base of one of the elevations.

We're not sure whether the huge beam across the centre of the room was here during the Merchant's time. If not, it arrived soon after, in the early–mid 16th century. Supported on huge, heavy corbel stones, its installation – without the aid of modern mechanical equipment – must have been a huge feat.

The Wall Paintings

The colourful stars, flowers and other paintings – possibly reminiscent of contemporary wallpaper designs – date from the late 18th or early 19th century. It's likely they were painted freehand and applied in *secco-fresco* technique. This is where pigments are mixed with an organic binder, such as size or casein, and applied onto dry plaster. At Tudor Merchant's House, this plaster was undoubtedly made of lime, sand and hair (see page 26).

Honesty's the best policy

By 1500, merchants should have been relatively trustworthy. However, a few years earlier that wasn't always the case. In the late 15th century, it was discovered that merchants had been adding gravel and sawdust to spices, including nutmeg. So in 1493, the London Grocers' Company employed men known as 'garbellers' to inspect spices as they came into port. If they weren't up to scratch, the merchant was locked in stocks and the offending spices burned under their nose.

Above left The Trading Area at the entrance to the house, where the Merchant would have displayed his wares to passing visitors

The Kitchen

The servants' domain, this room was a hive of activity. Large pots and a spit hung in the room-dominating fireplace, above a fire that was always burning.

Here bread was baked, soup warmed, and meats boiled or roasted. Fish and bacon dried in the chimney as the cook prepared fruit and vegetables for dinner. The meat on the spit was turned by a Focarius, usually a young boy. He may also have created tallow candles, or 'rushlights,' by dipping wicks into the hot fat dropped from the meat.

Come nightfall, all the household's servants would have slept around the huge fireplace, bunked down in beds made of turf; with the exception perhaps of the manservant, who would sleep on the first floor as a first line of defence against intruders. The lady's maid may have also had the privilege of sleeping in the bedroom, ready for when her mistress was in need of anything. Soup and drinks were kept warm throughout the night, in case the Merchant and his family fancied a midnight snack.

Above The Aumbry cupboard, where leftover food would be kept for the poor, with the family's wine barrels below

Life in service

On becoming teenagers, it was time for young Tudors to choose a career. Some took on apprenticeships, spending at least seven years learning trades such as carpentry and goldsmithery and eventually setting themselves up as a qualified tradesmen. For most (around 70%) there was little choice. They entered service, where they received food, lodgings and a small wage, and learnt from their elders. Relationships between servants and masters varied: some stayed with the same family for many years, while other households had a high turnover of staff.

The superstitious Tudors
In the kitchen

- Fire was generally thought to be lucky, as was spitting on a fire
- If a fire burst into full flame, an unexpected guest would arrive
- Knives should be sharpened after dark – or murderers might visit
- Knives in the kitchen should never be crossed

The furnishings

The Aumbry cupboard

This was where any food uneaten by the Merchant and his family was stored. In the evening, homeless and jobless locals could ask to be fed from any leftovers that hadn't already been earmarked by the household staff.

Riven oak furniture

The stand for the large table, the benches and some of the stools in this room are all made from one of the most commonly used Tudor woods, riven oak. This is wood that has been left to dry out, forming small cracks. It can then be easily peeled apart and cut to size without a saw. Because it's dried out, it doesn't buckle or deform after you've started to use it.

The barrel chair

Although a replica, this chair demonstrates an early form of recycling: it was originally a container.

The meal arch

Used to store things such as flour, this oak chest could be described as an early version of flatpack furniture. It was designed to be easily taken apart for treatment or transportation. The lid, which can be turned over and is fitted with small grooves, could also have been used for making bread.

The meat safe

The box hanging from the beam-laden ceiling was – as its name suggests – used for keeping meat safe from flies, spiders and insects. It's made of lime-washed oak, lime being a minor antibacterial substance. Underneath would have been drying herbs and lavender, whose scent deterred pests. This particular safe is a replica, made for Tudor Merchant's House in 2010 by Paul Northwood.

Right Warm up by the open fire in the Kitchen

How the room has changed

The ground floor was once entirely cut off from the rest of the building; the stairs you see today didn't exist, and the first floor was reached via steps on the outside of the building, on the side facing the sea (see illustration on page 3). It's likely that in 1500 the space now occupied by the stairs was where the servants slept.

Oranges and lemons…

Tenby Tudors were used to seeing lemons and limes arrive on ships from the Continent. However in 1566, a ship from Aveiro, Portugal brought to Tenby a fruit never seen before in Wales: oranges. It's said that a Portuguese seaman had to explain to the bemused Welshman what to do with them. They were the first documented oranges in Wales.

The Latrine Tower,
The Herb Garden

The Latrine Tower

Most Tudor toilets were very basic. You might have a hole in the ground outside the back door, or chamber pots that were manually emptied into a cesspit. In contrast, the Latrine – or garderobe – Tower at Tudor Merchant's House is luxurious. Not only are there three indoor toilets, but each also has a seat.

Although there was a toilet on each floor, these were staggered. This is because, with no complex pipes and plumbing systems, excrement was washed straight down. By staggering the latrines, each could be used at the same time without risk of an unwanted 'gift' from above.

Stories from the cesspit

All that waste had to go somewhere: underneath the tower is a 1.3-metre deep cesspit. In 1984, this was excavated by the Dyfed Archaeological Trust. Their findings, published five years later in the *Bulletin of the Board of Celtic Studies*, not only reveal more about the tower's workings, but also the lives of those who lived and worked at Tudor Merchant's House.

They proved that, although the tower was a later addition, it was almost certainly here in Tudor times. Pottery shards discovered, including a vessel from Spain or Portugal, two north Devon ware jars and the remains of two bronze pins, all date from around the late 16th century. (Interestingly only one shard came from west Wales, suggesting just how much must have been imported.)

Findings also showed that the cesspit was lined with sawdust, used to absorb excess fluids. On top was an organic layer, which included household waste. It would have been 'flushed' by a spring, which ran from the back of the house to the front. However the pit wasn't huge and it's likely it still needed emptying manually, probably around once a year. This was perhaps with the aid of a 'Gong farmer', someone whose unenviable job it was to clean cesspits, and who was only allowed to work at night.

But perhaps most fascinating is the insight provided into the varied diet enjoyed by those who lived here. Traces of at least 11 herb varieties, 13 different fruits (both local and imported) and the bones of 15 fishes and birds were all found, as well as oats, wheat and barley. However the inhabitants' health wasn't always top notch: evidence of human roundworm and whipworm were also discovered. *(See page 19 for more on the Tudor diet).*

Above The Latrine Tower as seen from the Hall Chamber. With three, seated indoor toilets, it was the height of bathroom luxury in Tudor times

The Herb Garden

It's quite likely that the Merchant's wife spent her days searching fields and lanes for wild herbs and plants, bringing them back to this, then larger, space. The plants you see today replicate those the Merchant's wife might have grown: amongst others, there are cornflowers, chives, common jasmine, common lavender, daisies, marigolds, oregano, rosemary, and the red rose of Lancaster and white of York.

Right Detail of the herb garden, behind the Kitchen

Below A woodcut from *The Grete Herbal*, 1526. This was the first fully illustrated herbal encyclopedia, detailing the medicinal properties of plants

The superstitious Tudors
The hangman

- It was said to be good luck to touch a man who was was about to be hanged – and the rope used was said to be a good cure for headaches

Everyday uses of plants

Tudors used plants for dyeing clothes, in cooking and also for medicines. Known as 'simples', these plant-based remedies were hugely important at the time. Girls were taught to mix them from a young age, and herbals – books full of remedies and the medicinal properties of plants – such as Richard Banckes's *Herball* (published in 1525) and *The Grete Herball* (1526) were frequently reprinted.

Some Tudor remedies are still used today: chamomile and lavender to calm; peppermint to soothe the stomach. Others are less familiar. Rosemary was thought good for headaches and to help enhance memory; it would often be seen at weddings, to aid the bride in remembering her vows, and funerals, to help remember the dead.

The Hall Chamber

This impressive room was where the Merchant's family lived, worked and received visitors. As the stairs would not have been here, they would have entered through the external door, just visible behind the curtain to the right of the fireplace. At meal times, this was where food was brought from the kitchen below.

Here, in air sweetened with herbs (strewn not only for their pleasing scent but also to discourage the Plague) the Merchant did sums at his writing desk while his children learned musical instruments or played games, such as Nine Men's Morris, Fox and Geese, and Jacks. His wife may have been receiving guests with *piment*, a popular Pembrokeshire red wine-like drink, served piping hot and spiced with ginger, cinnamon and honey.

Right   The writing desk in the Hall Chamber

Below   The Hall Chamber, looking towards the beautifully carved chairs at the top table, where the Merchant and his wife would sit

The wall decor

On entering this room, guests would have immediately been aware of the family's political leanings. On the wall are hangings in the Tudor livery colours of green and cream, alerting guests that the family were followers of Henry VII, not Richard III.

The Tudor rose also features in the room, in the colourful yellow frieze lining the top of the wall. Other images within the painting replicate those on bosses in Tenby Church, showing that the family were good church people, while boats highlight the Merchant's maritime links. There's also a mermaid. In 1500, the Tenby Mermaid was a positive symbol of good luck but 50 years later it would take on an altogether different meaning, becoming the sign of a brothel.

Changing status

In medieval South Pembrokeshire, rooms such as this were the preserve of the wealthiest men. Houses with a hall on the first floor were usually built for defensive purposes. By the 1500s, the design was being adopted by the middle classes – people like the Merchant and other well-off tradesmen – but was falling out of favour with the rich. As a result, such dominating rooms were no longer a status symbol, but having your main living room on the first floor was still preferable to having it at ground level (Tudor streets were far from clean).

The 'trip step'

The stairs here lead to the only bedroom above, the Bedchamber (see page 20). However watch out for the 4th one up. The 'trip step' – which would have stuck out a little, not being as deep – was designed to catch unwanted and unsuspecting guests off guard, so the family would be alerted to their presence. You can still see the mark of the original step underneath the banisters.

The Welsh flag
If you rotate the green and white stripes of the wall hangings 90 degrees they reflect the background of the Welsh flag. This flag – including the fiery red dragon, a symbol of Wales since at least 830AD – was used by Henry VII at the Battle of Bosworth in 1485. However it wasn't until 1959 that it was officially recognised as the national flag of Wales.

Above Visitors are welcome to try out popular Tudor games laid out on the table in the Hall Chamber

Above Left The Tenby mermaid adorns the fireplace in the Bedchamber. Originally a symbol of good luck, it later took on a very different meaning, becoming the sign of a brothel

The dining area

At around 11am each day, the family and their guests gathered at the board table for their main meal.

Although this might seem early to us, the Tudors had no electricity and worked around the sun, so would have been busy since dawn. By 11am, they were surely ready for a hearty meal.

Laying the table

The table would have been set with a red woollen 'borde-clothe' and covered by two white linen 'napes' – using fewer than two or re-using one was considered to invite death. Upon these cloths would have been set dishes next to knives and shallow, wide spoons laid upside-down so as to not let the devil sit in them. As forks weren't used at the time, most food was eaten by hand. The right was reserved for eating, while the cleaner left was used to take items from the table, such as dried nuts and fruits placed in saucers and dotted around.

The Tudors were obsessed with using material goods to signify status (there were even Sumptuary Laws, which dictated what you could wear based on your class); crockery was no exception. The Merchant would have splashed out on pewter trenchers and finely carved pewter knives for himself and his very best guests. Visitors of 'average' standing might have used ones with fine bone handles. Everyone else would have had to make do with wooden utensils.

The table also features brown pots, a common sight in Tudor homes. These aren't originals, but are very similar to ones we think the family would have used. They were made by John Hudson, a specialist in reproduction pottery, based on shards found in the latrine tower during the 1984 excavation (see page 14).

Seating arrangements

The Merchant, and perhaps his wife, would have sat in the beautifully carved wooden chairs at the head of the table. It's possible they could be Welsh in origin, but their design isn't typical of the area, so it's more likely that they came from Portugal. The family's guests would have sat on chests and cushions.

Keeping clean

As he took his place, the Merchant would have placed a napkin over his top. His male servants slung napkins across their shoulders, with the ladies donning aprons. Clothes and materials were expensive, and even the wealthy only had a few changes of outfit. As the best way to clean clothes was by hanging them in the latrine for a few days steeped in ammonia (thought to kill nits and lice), every effort was made to keep them as blemish-free as possible.

The superstitious Tudors
At dinner

- Spilt salt should be thrown over the left shoulder to blind the devil, and not your guardian angel on the right

Below Bread was a staple of the Tudor diet, and was creamier, denser and chewier than the bread eaten today

What did they eat?

For rich and poor, bread took a central role in meals. Though, unlike our modern bread, that which the merchant's family ate would have been denser, chewier and creamier in colour. For those strapped for cash, a lower order brown bread was available, if you didn't mind not knowing exactly what went in it, the most common ingredient being sawdust. What part of the bread you received also had social connotations. Bread would be cut horizontally; the 'upper crust' was sliced for the Merchant's family, while the ash-covered 'dole' was given to the servants and begging poor.

Meat was a preserve of the wealthy, and the family who lived here enjoyed a variety. The excavation of the Latrine Tower found traces of bones from cattle, sheep and goats. Perhaps unsurprisingly considering Tenby's location, the family also enjoyed plenty of seafood including lobster, oyster, crab and barnacle. For the less affluent, vegetarian options appear to have included an abundance of fruit, both local – such as berries, damsons and apples – and imported, such as figs, grapes and raisins.

These ingredients likely made up typically Tudor dishes, such as lamb cawl (a traditionally Welsh one-pot a bit like a broth or stew) *chykens in Hoccee* (chickens stuffed with grapes) or *Wardonys in syryp* (pears in wine syrup).

Food was probably accompanied with beer, wine, sherry ('sack'), mead and cider – often because water wasn't safe to drink unless boiled. Whenever the Merchant wanted his glass refilled, servants would have first washed it. The Merchant would have drunk the refilled liquid immediately; there was a deep-rooted fear in society that languishing glasses would be poisoned.

Right The top table laid out
for a meal in the Hall Chamber

The Bedchamber

As darkness drew in, the Merchant and his family retired to bed. The whole family and any guests would have crowded into this one room, sleeping below the wooden beams.

Fortunately, the room would have been bigger then – around the same size as the Hall Chamber below. The dividing wall that now separates this room from the staff office is a relatively recent addition.

Sleeping arrangements

Adults took to the bed, while their children – possibly seven or eight of them – slept on palliasses: thin, scratchy mattresses made from straw, sawdust or seaweed and placed on the floor. Babies arguably had the most comfortable option, with a crib to themselves (unless they were a twin).

The main bed was not just for the Merchant and his wife. It might hold up to six people and they would have shared with their adult guests, whether close family members or visiting merchants. Although this might seem like an uncomfortable arrangement to us today, it was not long since most people had slept on the floor, on rush matting. Presumably even squeezing into a bed with five others was far preferable. Tudors also slept sitting up; so as to discourage a visit from the Angel of Death, who might think they had died.

The bed

The bed would have been roped and covered in the nicest material the family could afford, probably flannel. The one here is not original, but was made in 1987, carved from an oak tree that fell on the Dolaucothi estate during the Great Storm.

Tudor families

Although Tudors had a number of children – one a year on average – approximately 25% died before they were four; the first year being the most dangerous.

Those lucky enough to survive into childhood helped around the house from a young age; by four or five you might be looking after younger siblings, or helping your mother with weeding and feeding pigs. In a house such as this, the Merchant's children would have been educated at home, or better still, placed with similar families to encourage new trading links. In 1500, few children went to school; if the Merchant's children did go, it would most likely have been only the boys, and they would have learnt Arithmetic, Divinity (RE) and Latin. In the coming years, increased importance was placed on schooling, particularly by the new Welsh King and Queen. Consequently while only 5% of men and 1% of women could write in 1500, by the end of the century this figure had increased to 25% and 10% (though Londoners were disproportionately literate).

Left   The Bedchamber

Above right   Window in the Bedchamber with views overlooking Tenby harbour

Tudor women

Tudor housewives helped educate their children and run the household. The Merchant's wife would have assisted with business matters, ensured the best quality food was brought home from market and mended clothes and tapestries. Some widows ran businesses independently. In her spare time, the Merchant's wife might have taken walks with friends and neighbours, or watched the comings and goings in the harbour from the window in this room, which looks out over Bridge Street – then the only route to the sea for horses and carts. When her husband was away, she may have sat at the window, waiting for him to walk back to their front door – safely returned from sea.

Swaddling

At the time, babies were kept away from trouble by being 'swaddled' in cloth and hung against the wall. After around three or four months old, they were able to have their arms outside the tightly wrapped binding. You can have a go at swaddling using the doll in this room and the pegs above – the doll is christened Robert after one of Tenby's most famous residents, Robert Recorde (see page 8).

The Decline and Rise of Tenby

By the end of the 17th century, Tenby was no longer a prosperous port town.

Tenby built its fortune on trade and fishing. But after 1600, foreign wars and the development of boats with keels halted much of the lucrative sea trade; when the tide is out for half the day, a boat with a keel would fall over if it was sitting on sand. At the same time, neighbouring Narberth and Pembroke grew as market towns, presenting competition, and fishermen from the west of England gained increased control over fish stocks.

The English Civil War brought further misfortune: the town underwent sieges and battles, fluctuating between Parliamentary and Royalist control. Consequently, many residents died or were taken prisoner (the five cannons on Castle Hill are from this period). Then in 1650–51, a devastating plague wiped out half the population. With nobody left to trade with, merchants in Tenby abandoned their homes and businesses; many relocated to Bristol where they had family and business links, in order to continue working.

Over the next century, Tenby was left to ruin. 'Pigs roam among the abandoned houses and Tenby presents a dismal spectacle,' wrote John Wesley, founder of the Methodist Church, at the end of the 18th century. In fact, in 1784 there were so many wild pigs that the Council appointed two constables just to contain them.

'Within these Walls are the most compleat Ruins of an Old Town'

A visitor to Tenby in 1767

Top *The Tenby Prawn Seller* by William Powell Frith, 1880

Top A Great Western Rail poster for Tenby. When the railway opened in 1863, tourism in the town boomed

Bottom *Lexden Terrace* by Charles Smith Allen

Birth of a seaside resort

In the late 18th and early 19th century overseas wars deterred wealthy Georgians from travelling to Europe. This fuelled a subsequent increase in British domestic tourism. It appears Tenby benefitted, beginning to attract holidaymakers looking for sand and sea: mentions of recreational bathing and strangers visiting the beach date back to 1767. Despite this, the town itself remained in a poor state.

The regeneration begins

In 1805, the wealthy Sir William Paxton moved into what is now Tenby House, near the centre of town. Soon after, he commissioned an engineer and architect to help him undertake what would become his largest investment project: creating a 'fashionable bathing establishment suitable for the highest society'. A building on the quayside was converted into bath houses, with accommodation and a coach house alongside. He remodelled the road linking the harbour and town, and funded and built two reservoirs to overcome the water shortages often experienced in summer.

Some were sceptical about Tenby's regeneration: 'experience must decide whether the present attempts to raise it on a level with the older, larger and better established bathing places are judicious' noted resident artist Charles Norris (see page 24) in 1812. But work continued with the support of the Town Council. By the mid-1850s, Tenby had a theatre, markets stocked with fresh food and luxury products, a circulating library, and formal promenades on which you could 'see and be seen'. In 1836, Middle Row was razed to open up Tudor Square and two years later the Tenby Improvement Act resulted in improvements to infrastructure.

Growth continued into the latter half of the century and beyond; the town expanded beyond its medieval walls, pastel-coloured hotels springing up along the cliff front. In 1863 the railway opened, bringing further influxes of tourists. In May 1898, the Duchess of York officially opened the Royal Victoria Pier (since demolished), encouraging steamboats to bring even more visitors, including those hoping to cure medical problems and naturalists hunting for fossils. Visitors explored shorelines and caves, listened to bands on Castle Hill and relaxed in horse-drawn bathing machines on the seafront. Tenby had developed into a seaside resort much like the one people flock to today.

Beatrix at Tenby
In 1900, Beatrix Potter stayed in No 2 The Croft overlooking North beach; the garden pond features in *The Tale of Peter Rabbit*.

'I went into the town this morning to buy something and then came out onto the pier, when I was surprised and delighted to see a great big man-of-war in the bay. It had come in round the corner and anchored to land stores for the coastguard'

Beatrix Potter's letter to her cousin Evie, 24 April 1900

Saving Tudor Merchant's House

In the early 20th century, there was renewed interest in the fast-deteriorating 'Old House' on the way to the quayside.

It was a house of little importance for many years. By 1867, it was connected to next door – the building that now houses the Plantagenet restaurant – and divided into tenements that were presumably poorly looked-after. The now blocked interconnecting doors between the two buildings can still be seen inside Tudor Merchant's House on the first floor.

Then in July 1930, C.R. Peers paid a visit to Tenby. Peers was Chief Inspector of Ancient Monuments for England, Scotland and Wales and President of the Society of Antiquaries, and he immediately recognised the importance of repairing the old building. 'The need for repair... is a very real and urgent one' he wrote. 'The house is a rare survival of a medieval building, is of exceptional importance, and should on every account be carefully preserved.'

The town debates

In September of that year, a Town Council meeting was held to discuss the house's future. It appeared at least £6–800 would be needed to complete the necessary works (about £35–45,000 today); a project for which there was no public funds. However, recognising the importance of preserving the house, it was thought the funds could be raised through loans or grants. It appears most were amenable to this plan, but some thought the costs a little excessive – one attendee highlighted that you could build a new house for the same amount.

The proposal to repair the house was not entirely popular with all of Tenby's residents either. One, known only as 'Indignant Ratepayer', wrote to the *Western Mail* in frustration: 'if the preservation of the ramshackle house were going to be of material benefit to Tenby, add to its popularity or bring in revenue then there might be some sense in the proposal... But as a resident of nearly forty years standing... I do not hesitate to say that in the course of the summer season not a score of visitors exhibit any interest in the "Old House".' Others disagreed; in response, Herbert M. Vaughan wrote to the *Tenby and County News*, stating that 'The Old House has been a prominent and beloved landmark of Tenby for at least two generations' (16 September, 1930). Vaughan disagreed with the 'Indignant Ratepayer's' statement that visitors weren't interested, suggesting it could make for an interesting museum. 'Tenby Museum's curator, Arthur L. Leach, agreed, pointing out that while other medieval buildings in the area existed, most of the former households of merchants, townsmen and sea-tradesmen had been 'swept away or ruined architecturally' (October 1930). Although the Old House had been changed inside – modern fireplaces and windows installed, for example – the exterior was still very much intact. Leach even suggested it could be done out to look as it might have appeared in 1500 – exactly what we have done with it today.

Bottom Tudor Merchant's House lies tucked down a narrow, Norman alley and was once connected with the building next door, now the Plantagenet restaurant

Opposite A postcard entitled *Old House in the Five Arches*, Tenby

Saving the 'Old House'

And so, from 1930–8, through public appeal and subscriptions, the funds were slowly raised to save the house. Half of these subscriptions came from local sources, and the other half through the Pilgrim and National Trusts, along with a private contribution from Tenby Museum & Art Gallery. Pre-eminent figures were key in encouraging donations, such as architect Sir Bertram Clough Williams-Ellis, who wrote to newspapers highlighting the state the house was in. Philanthropist and chocolate maker George Cadbury, who was known for investing in historic buildings to save them from destruction, also contributed. It was through their efforts that the funds were raised to purchase the house.

The National Trust also asked the Town Council to vest the house in the charity, as they would be willing to contribute to repairs under certain conditions. The then-owners of the house were two sisters, Clara Jane Isabel and Bettina Gordon Canning. In November 1937, they were contacted regarding the Trust's request. They agreed, and the following year Tudor Merchant's House was donated to the National Trust.

Renovating the house

Work on renovations began soon after the house came into the Trust's care. A floor installed in the 18th and 19th centuries. was removed, and replaced with one made of concrete, 35 centimetres thick (this was removed and replaced with another concrete floor in 1984). Excavation work was carried out on the chimney, during which it was discovered that its original features had been destroyed in the late 19th century, when a door and drain were 'smashed through'. The cesspit was also excavated. In 1951, the hard work paid off when the building was awarded a Grade I-listed status.

'The Old House has been a prominent and beloved landmark of Tenby for at least two generations'
Herbert M Vaughan, 1930

Looking After Tudor Merchant's House today

A team of dedicated staff and volunteers help make this former Merchant's house the vibrant, special place it is today; where visitors are encouraged to dress up in Tudor costume, play games in the Hall Chamber, or have a go at swaddling 'Robert' the doll.

Working with the community

It is also, in part, thanks to the local community and council that Tudor Merchant's House is still standing here. We continue to work closely together, particularly with groups such as the WI, Probus and the University of the Third Age, as well as gardening clubs and other visiting groups. The community regularly gives its support; in 2012 and 2016, the Tenby Male Voice Choir sung for us at St Mary's Parish Church.

Dressing up

You'll often find us donning replica Tudor dress. Bringing the house to life, it also helps to spread the word and celebrate important occasions. 2016, for instance, was the 450th anniversary of the first documented oranges being brought into Wales through Tenby. We celebrated by playing games outside the house in full costume, and were joined by mace bearers, two of our merchants and even the Mayor.

Blooming marvellous

In 2016, although we didn't enter Tenby in Bloom ourselves, we were asked by the town clerk if the judges could come and visit the property and take a look at the herb garden. Of course we said yes!

Top   A volunteer and costumed interpreter dressing the elaborately carved bed in the Bedchamber

Right   A detail of the wall paintings in the Trading Area

Left   A young visitor dresses up to explore the house

Conservation

After all the efforts that were taken to restore Tenby's 'Old House', we know it's important we look after it carefully to ensure it stays in a good condition, for ever for everyone.

On a regular basis, staff at Tudor Merchants House practise conservation housekeeping in order to maintain the property and displays. We keep an eye on dust, damp and pests such as moths that might eat our woollen wool hangings. We monitor the environment carefully – you'll see humidistats placed around the house, there to measure temperature and humidity to ensure it's optimum for keeping the property in prime condition.

The conservation of the wall paintings

A key conservation focus for us has been protecting the historic wall paintings in the main entrance of the house. As you walk into the reception area, you'll notice a three-colour floral pattern adorning three of the walls.

The authentic artwork is thought to date to between the late 18th and early 19th century, with expert pigment analysis indicating that high quality materials were used to create the original freehand design.

In spring 2017, we undertook essential work on the north wall to stabilise the structure and preserve the paintings for future generations to enjoy. As part of the process, our conservators also examined the other walls in the entrance room and made a new discovery; more of the floral design exists under the modern-day plaster.

Peeling back the layers of time is just the start. We're now on a journey to learn more about the paintings; when exactly were they created and who was the artist behind the delicate piece?

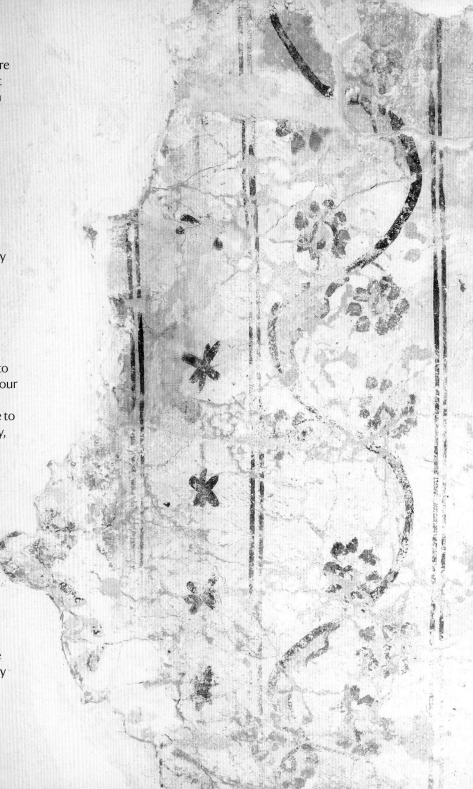

The Artists
of Tenby

Since its earliest days, Tenby has been the subject of both art and literature.

Charles Norris (1779–1858)
In 1805, Norris and his family moved into a house down the road from Tudor Merchant's. In the following years they witnessed the beginnings of the town's transformation from dilapidated abandonment to fashionable summer resort.

Norris documented this transformation through his topographical ink and watercolour drawings, producing almost 300 illustrations just of Tenby. They make up some of the best records of the town in the early 19th century: the demolition of Middle Row in 1836; ships and boats in the harbour; Tudor Square crammed with cottages, a market and the town cross. Much of his work is now in the collections of Tenby Museum & Art Gallery.

Even though Charles became ill towards the end of his life, his granddaughter suggested that he continued to make sketches. He is buried with his second wife in Tenby cemetery.

> 'To the painter, the naturalist and the antiquary, few places can be more productive of gratification'
>
> Charles Norris on Tenby, in 1812

Above *Ancient Cottage Near Market Place* by Charles Norris, 1812

Margaret Mackinlay
Published in 1982, Margaret Mackinlay's book *Sage Peveril* takes place in the Tudor Merchant's House. Set in the Tudor period, it tells the story of a young woman who finds herself newly widowed at the same time that one of Francis Drake's captains arrives in Tenby.

> 'Below me, the small harbour lay dimly outlined by a waxing moon, which busily hurried between the storm-tossed clouds'
>
> Extract from Margaret Mackinlay's *Sage Peveril*, 1982

Augustus John (1878–1961)
The Tenby-born painter was one of the leading portrait artists of the 1920s. He spent his childhood in Tenby, attending a grammar school on Greenhill Road, but moved away to study at the Slade School of Art, London, when he was 17.

A social campaigner
During his 12 years in Tenby, Norris was also keenly involved in town politics and the education of the town's poor. In the 1830s, on discovering the Mayor had diverted the town's Poor Rate to electioneering and an annual dinner, Norris began protesting against the neglect of Tenby's residents, and the poor state of the town's sanitation system.